hardPressed Dual Poets Reader: Three

hardPressed Dual Poets Reader: Three

Maurice Scully
Jordi Valls Pozo / Translations by Raoul Izzard

Published by hardPressed poetry, Ireland
http://hardpressedpoetry.blogspot.com/
hardpressedpoetry@gmail.com

Acknowledgments

A version of 'Path' appeared in an online festschrift for Tony
Frazer's 60th birthday: tonyfrazer.weebly.com

The Current and Mother's Maiden Name appeared in 'Poetry
Wales' Summer 2017

GAME ON

Maurice Scully

PATH

A dog came up the steps with a tennis ball in its mouth to
shake itself dry. On my way back from the disused lighthouse
at the head of the pier I notice now he's still there &
alone & nosing the ball in quick crafty shifts towards the
edge then grabbing it back in its mouth several times just
in time until he lets the ball quite deliberately slip over &
fall down again into the water. Again. The future. Consilience.
And so our dog is in the water again after the ball. Now. Good dog.

PLACED

"where motley etc ... "

Plastic disk
laughs into
its cup.

The plastic
flat primary
colour of it.

The green
disk blinks
into its cup.

Don't let
the cup
tumble.

Dice tickle
the board.
Flick.

Slim textures
in circles squares
diamonds cylinders –

I heard
you rang
you answered
you

you parked
in the park
you too parked
next to the park

roof
roof-roof
roof-roof-roof

disk by disk
the cups open
uplaugh
      down to

your turn where
slap here's the cup.
Circle.
      Square.

Facts split
the picture
open.

Rice-grains
dimple the
ridges.

Mirrors
shimmer into
out there – *howaya!*
[Bang-bang].

But that was
the past the sea
of the past the
fog of the past

a forest of following
hollowing futures
bobbing whens
plastics pierced.

O co memor
or emco morat
may by water
vat or em

rald grass.
Brush past.
Trapped stick.
Red splash.

Spread low
with many
mythologies

rippling
a language's
underparts
tapping yr

fingers
quietly
to another
rhythm –

watch them
now focusing
what's to be said
& how

POOL

Turned down radio
laptop
& the day's

to-do list took tea
to work – hot –
into the cool shed in

the garden among
books   papers
beginning birdsong
in branches

tinkling down
to the brink
of spring …

Well you
might as well
live I too dislike it
the emperor

of ice cream bangs
with his bag full
of god dancing
in the moonlight

shimmering fangs
a blur slipping over
water in twilight
become a swan.

Marks. Dabs.
Misunderstandings.

That tall stillness
a heron. So
far so good

among golden
daffodils a rooky
wood

a solitary reaper
a guy with a guitar
my tippet
(only tulle)

now that I look
now that the
hunt is on –

kin –
    cash –
          peace –

a shiver in
the grass where
breezes passed

& speckled
possibility dipped
a wing

dark-money!
          stark-monkey!
dancing on
trees on leaves

landing on tilting
turning the last the
least the pages dust
rising to but

to get to/down/
this (must)
that persistent

piece (down) of/
whose birthday
is it anyway?
& what is it

to what is it *time*
to throw away
(this must be)

next? this must
be the way back
yellowing glints
a tremendous fish

to whispers build-
ing in the little breezes
between this & this
darkness on yr desk

on the open
surface of yr
dark one leaf landing
dark on dark

imprinted this –
stark – come in –
hey! – thanks –
it's started –

park yr cart outside
the park in the heart
of the city pierced by
a startled barking

bringing you
just so far through
all that

to here to now.
Down. Where the Here
& the Now sit still.
Arc. Huge irregular

segments. Parts. Tested.
A whirr of wings.
Where fire works.
Welcome.

PEP

Pour drain-block into
it to let its thick acid
eat a passage through
it through it then wash
with hot water for the flow.

Maguire & Paterson
Fireside Safety Matches
average contents 220, item.
Strike away from body.
Mind the gap, then patch it.

Hey presto.

PATCH

Meanwhile
back at the
studio

time tight
taking another
20 A5 sheets

of paper
touch each
one on
your desk

with yr right
middle
finger &
have them

touched
each one
by yr
assistant –

once – with
the *left index*.
Tick-tick.
Do.

The left. Lightly. Got that?
Document the action.
Collaboration.
Opus II.

Sip coffee.
Click fingers.
Tap a table.
Take notes.

Hot.

An apple
on a napkin
on a desk.

Apparently
our climate
is much more
sensitive to

small forces
than had
previously been
imagined.

A hammer bangs
& its echoes
angle
back.

Wearing a
blindfold
touch what you
imagine you

can. Tick.
Sign. Number.
Document
the action.

Chance operations.
A fan? Opus III.
Time's
tight.

The processes that are
self-augmenting
convert
a

little ripple of temperature variations –
apparently our
climate's much more

sensitive to minute
forces – converting
slight ripples
times

temperatures
to powerful variation-waves that
gather size apparently
momentum climate

decades or even centuries
flowing on into the
future until some major

appearance of our
much more sensitive
to small forces than had

previously been/between
my fingers & *hey!* some
countervailing
force stops it.

Ars longa
vita brevis/

So.

Touch a page.
It touches back
snap & whisper it
reaches back to you –

who? You report it. It
stays. Glazed. Phased.
At the Busy Intersection
of Acorn & Art-Art.

And shame us
with a repeated
pun. Fun? Dash.

Black. We touch a
page; it touches back.
How much? *All!* Cage.
Light. Knack. Pool.

Plastic disk snaps on
the rim of another disk
so that it flips bright &
lands square

with a click in the pot –
you win.

PARED

a can on
a table
its label

torn beside
an apple with
a bit gone
just here

comma

red
green
brown(ish)

sugary
curlicues

> drop
> of
> coffee
> sliding
> over a
> cup's
> lip
> gather
> ing
> at its
> base.
> quiet.

ripple
in the
palm leaves

pod pendant
from a
spent flower

burst of
buddleia
snakes of
bindweed

tickle of
daisies

undersplash of
cyclamen *froth*
of appleblossom

clustered on
purple white-green
wings on tight

florets crisp
heaps in corners
leaves & shadows

all that –

stones
settled down in to
into fissures under-
ground –

then a feeling
a/growing of
having –

water
is one of
the wonderful
things –

light mist
on window
clear snail-trail
through it –

weeds of
instigations
ivy of
cling-cling –

all chilly
& alone &
mistaking

yet more
mistakes
for the one

true take
that feeling
a *new* feeling
growing

o god
of having
powerless

written
quite enough
at yr age now
thank you

– splash!

go the colours
as they hit
surface

at force
out of
the blue

snowberry
dock nettle
& haw

talking to
you listening
to or
waiting to

or   &
or   I
if   then

o

PART

Details
trickle in to
the story &
fill it. Listen.

Rain on the glass
of the window
switching direction.
There you go.

Snap. Look: a life –
a packet of white envelopes –
nobody about –
dawn –

chill silhouettes
stopped in the air
condensing into the
first

daytime trees in
pale light. Perfect
information. No more
'gems'. Right?

One dewdrop
colliding with
& merging its
music into

two others in a
tiny tattoo of
imagined sound
as they swell &

fall while lines of
bright dots on a thin
appleskin here
fan out from its

black stem – look:
touch a button,
hear a voice –
darkness puckered –

a plume of flesh-pale
smoke on a pale blue sky –
whispers of yr pen on the
page as it brushes

& whisks –
this & then
this &
then

a swoop of dots
rising from the lagoon
densing – spreading – twisting –
sliding away

then back again then –
suddenly close – flitting over
the parapet of the bridge
a haze of whirling

beings from Siberia
to land in silence
on the other side …

Time to pack up & go
(you bet): Mace, Lace, Hats,
Tabard & Soluble Goo –
buy 1 –

get 2 – then take care –
& head off over a
bridge over a river
over a hill

emphatically off *that*
way: one apple
on a winter tree –
three white houses

in a field on a
matchbox, silver
light between a spinney
& a hedge. What date's today

anyway? Where am I?
Who? What? Who cares?
We're on the road again.

There you go.

POSIT

Elastic risk
factors into
its slot

drastic
slits in it
that

flatten
other mastic
pips

(don't let
  the bits
  crumble)

cusp

crumple up
the telling
wont. Can't.

Dice-grain ridges.
Brisk. False.
To know

the facts. Emerald.
Smile. Tell me
a little

something about
that. O blame
not the marl.

Splash. To split the
picture
open.

How circling
& descending
& singing & –

So.

Now a door opens
& a clock
ticks.

PITH

A dog came up the steps with a ball in his mouth &
shook himself dry. Then he put the ball down carefully
on the pier & began to nose it towards the edge,
grabbing it back before it fell over into the water.
Nobody on the pier seemed to notice it, nobody
seemed to be with it, the dog was absorbed in its
game, the day was absorbed in itself. After several little
runs like this combined with quick retrievals, the dog –
it was no accident – *let* the ball roll over & fall down
again into the water. Then he jumped in after the ball
with a great splash – different rules, different game,
different winners. There are laws & there are accidents,
one more powerful than the other, & there may be general
laws of accident-prediction (what in this context does
accident mean?), so that each drop falling over the history of
life laughs as it lands to break on water, dog, ball, stone,
interpretation … For whom then is the record made? Who
dominate, who persuade? And for how long? And what is
'the truth'? Out 'there'? Where? How? An idea came up the
steps with another idea in its mouth & shook itself dry. Now …

EVIL/ GUILLEM TELL
EVIL/ WILLIAM TELL

Jordi Valls Pozo
Translations by Raoul Izzard

LECTOR

Fes-hi un cop d'ull, val la pena perdre el temps
i no cal que t'ho pensis massa. Acosta-t'hi,
que a l'altra banda del paper hi ha silenci,
en arribar a la teva orella traspassa
el lleu brogit de la sordesa. Un altre
món on dissoldre't ve de la pau i torna
vibrant al mirall líric que crema l'ànima
per indefinició. El mot ferma el nus
d'un nou escenari. Amb tu, tot és possible.
Vés i proclama la passió on l'èxit no hi compta.

READER

Come on, it's worth your while;
don't overthink it. Closer,
there is silence on the paper's flip side,
and on reaching your ear, it crosses
the light rumour of deafness. Another world
where you give yourself to peace and return
vibrating to the lyric mirror that burns the soul
with indistinctness. The word tightens the knot
of a new scene. With you, everything is possible.
Come, proclaim a passion that slights success.

COGNOM DE MARE

Cada cop que m'aboco, m'hi llançaria
broc avall per atrapar l'ull profund
d'on vaig sortir. I dos ulls com dos pous,
l'indret on caure amb la pell diürna al fons.
Reconeixes l'infant, mare?

                      El tràngol
és comú i no sabem destriar-nos l'ànima
que es despenja i tanca la closca fora
del nucli que ens uneix, perquè és difícil
desdoblar-se on comença l'argument.
Tentinejo entre les arrels i perdo
l'instint per guanyar destresa, dos ulls
dins del meu vol absent, molt lluny del blau.
Sento l'espetec de la pedra al fons.

MOTHER'S SURNAME

Each time I peered in I would launch myself
from the wellhead to trap the keen eye
I had left behind. And two eyes like two wells,
the place they fell in daylight to the depths.
Do you recognise your child, mother?

                      The trance
is mutual and we don't know how to set aside soul
that unhooks, closing the shell outside
of the nucleus that joins us, because it hurts
to split into two when the argument starts.
I stagger between roots and I lose
the instinct to acquire skills, two eyes
inside on autopilot, far, far from the blue.
I hear a stone crack down below.

APOCALIPSI

Han fet les maletes i surten ja per la porta,
deixen la clau al pany −no la necessitaran
més-. Desesmats pugen al cotxe, marxen lluny
per carreteres secundàries.
                      Va arribant
l'hora justa quan s'ha de tancar el cercle.
Reposen sols en polígons industrials i defugen
els curiosos entre clapes de bosc, ocults.
Cap ànima pot destorbar-los, són més vells
encara que els més vells, i ara tornen asprívols,
en tenen prou amb el que han après i els fills tampoc
no han portat res de nou.
                      Després al desert desen
el cotxe i continuen caminant per les dunes;
fatigats van deixant peces de roba suada,
no els atemoreix la nuesa. I les maletes,
perfectament tancades, serveixen pel foc
a les gèlides nits. Arrupits l'un amb l'altre
ja res no els identifica, són el que diuen ser.
Més tard grunyen, no parlen, es van apropant.

Ella, no ho suporta més, torna la costella
i desapareix.
                      Ell, cansat, no veu l'arcàngel
que amb l'espasa li tusta el clatell, que l'ajup.

APOCALYPSE

They pack their cases and are out the door.
In the lock is the key they won't need
anymore. Car loaded, despondent they head off
for side roads.
                    The hour
when the circle seals is close.
They rest in industrial estates alone; concealed
among the woods, they shun the curious.
 No soul can bother them for they are older still
than the oldest, and return sullen,
sufficing with what is learnt, like children
 who bring back nothing new.
                              Later, through the desert,
they abandon the car and continue on foot over dunes.
Exhausted, they leave a trail of sweat-drenched clothes,
no longer afraid of their own nakedness. And the suitcases,
perfectly sealed, serve to fuel a fire
on a freezing night. Snuggled up one in the other,
no ID, they are who they say they are.
Much later, they growl, not speaking, inch closer.

At her wit's end, she returns the rib,
dissolves.
                    Exhausted, he overlooks the archangel
whose sword thrust to the neck subdues him.

DANTE

Aspires a ser breu, però ets fill dels cíclops,
no pots fer res més que servir-te de l'èpica.
El safareig de la mare n'és l'origen.
L'elaboració del fals passat que creix
als ulls del nen; la memòria versemblant.
Totes aquestes roques són la muntanya
bastida amb els fragments que distret retrobes
entre passions inventades de veïns mítics
que han estat afegides al sender. Puges
i al revolt baixes. No goses trencar el ritme
camp a través, encara que la sospita
és vigent. Fas tombs al voltant de la cleda.

DANTE

You aspire to be brief, but you are the cyclop's son.
You cannot refuse the draw of the epic.
Mother's laundry is your origin.
The creation of a false past that grows
in the eyes of a child: a credible memory.
All these rocks are the mountain
raised with fragments you find distracting
between the invented loves of mythic neighbours
that have been added to the path. You rise
and in a twist you fall. You dare not break the rhythm
of cross country, although you suspect it
is pertinent. You stumble closer to the sheepfold.

TÍTOL PROVISIONAL

S'enderroquen els blocs en bella sincronia,
un darrere l'altre, del barri a la ciutat,
de la ciutat als pulmons, i surt l'alenada
que tot ho emboira, el silenci més pregon,
la duna seca i el respirar que va cremant
la necrosi del cor encrostada a l'artèria,
ningú no s'ho espera, s'ha trencat l'encanteri.

Això s'acaba, nois, la festa grossa ve ara.

PROVISIONAL TITLE

They demolished the blocks in exquisite symphony,
one after another, from the hood to the city,
from the city to the lungs, emerging in breath
that clouds it all, the deepest silence,
the dry dune and the breath that burns
arteries caked in the heart's necrosis,
which nobody expects, which breaks the spell.

That's all folks, next up is the real party.

INTENSITAT

La vida vol el crim perfecte que es dilata
o s'escurça en l'anècdota de l'imprevist.

Hi ha moments, experiències gravades amb foc,
per cada pas memorable buidat de l'ull.

La flauta segueix els paràmetres del so,
la vibració dúctil que parpelleja el núvol.

INTENSITY

Life requires the perfect crime dilates
or shrinks in anecdote that's unforeseen.

There are moments, experiences that fire engraves
for each memorable step it erases from sight.

The flute follows parameters of sound,
the ductile vibration that blinks the cloud.

EL CORRENT   *A Marga*

Hi faré cap, no m'empenyis. Les flors
que naveguen riu avall no són nenúfars,
davallen fins topar amb els obstacles.
Un bany de llum les sotmet a la dansa
d'anar i venir entre el foc i l'aigua.
Jo hi vaig i no hi vaig, però tu, el riu.

THE CURRENT   *A Marga*

All in good time, don't press me. The flowers
that wind their way down river are not lily pads.
They drift downstream and bump into obstacles there.
A bath of light invites them to the dance
Of here and there, between the flame and water
I stay or I go, but you, the river.

LES MANS DE LA MARE JERÒNIMA DE LA FUENTE

Aquestes mans deformades per l'artritis
que havien patit l'escombra solitària
del convent, ningú no les va escalfar prou.
I entre detalls d'un blau poderós s'afermen
les venes a la llum.
                La grandesa és lletja,
es corseca imitant l'exemple dels sants
que subjecten l'amor amb la fe encesa.

És difícil comprendre d'on surt la por,
com li endureix les dolces faccions de dona.
Potser una nit va sentir la tendresa,
de qui, per compassió, no la va seduir.

THE HAND OF MOTHER JERÓNIMA DE LA FUENTE

These hands deformed by arthritis
suffered for the solitary broom
of the barely heated convent.
And between details of a blue power,
the veins cling to the light.
                Here grandeur is ugly,
it dries up as it imitates the saints,
and buckles love down with burning faith.

It is difficult to know where fear comes in,
how it endures the sweet factions of woman.
Maybe, a night arrived when tenderness was felt
for whom, out of compassion, did not seduce her.

BACHUS AND ARIADNA A LA NATIONAL GALLERY

La fúria del sàtir lligat per serps
és més real que l'anglesa que em trepitja.
Tu no n'has de fer res de l'ull de poll,
no forma part del botí de Dionis.
La sala és a vessar d'experts precoços
on el blau marí i el del cel busquen fondre's
en cada turista; la veu del guia
que sovint confon el motiu amb la forma
exerceix d'autoritat narrativa.
Ariadna pragmàtica accepta el tracte.
Teseu, és massa lluny per rectificar
i Naxos una illa sense més oferta.
Quan es buida la sala, m'encalces lleugera,
i m'apresses perquè no arribem.
Els felins obedients tiren del carro.
Del mal de peus ningú més se'n fa càrrec.
Marxem com si mai no haguéssim vingut.
I sempre erres l'enunciat de l'enigma.

BACCHUS AND ARIADNE IN THE NATIONAL GALLERY

The fury of the satyr bound with serpents
is more real than the Englishwoman who tramples me.
What do you care for the callus on my foot?
It is not numbered among the spoils of Dionysius.
The gallery is full of precocious experts
where sea-blue and heaven seek to blend
with each tourist; the voice of the guide
that often confuses motive with form
exercises narrative authority.
Pragmatic Ariadne accepts the treaty.
Theseus is too far away to rectify
and Naxos, is an island with little to offer.
When the room empties, I draw near,
and it rewards me because we do not reach.
The obedient felines pull the cart.
Nobody worries about the pain in my feet.
We march on as if we'd never come
and always err in the riddle's wording.

LLENGUA TALLADA

llengua tallada al terra grumolls de sang és una flor
que t'estimo i mirem el riu més vermell
no hi ha paraules ni boca no hi ha paraules
i et mors per oblidar la terra insomne

llengua tallada amb gust de sal plores amor meu
una llum flor del desert mires al terra desolat
i digerim la sang oblidada digerim la sang
perquè tu m'abandones oblidat desert
altre cop a la boca

llengua tallada al terra desert de crepuscle
la mort que mires és l'estèril llavor sense tu
no sóc res mort darrera mort davallem i davallem
sense el record no hi ha paraules com no hi ha ulls
sense pupil·la al desert només mires absort
les dilatades ombres de la sang quallada

CUT TONGUE

Cut tongue on the floor blobs of blood a flower is
I love you and we observe the reddest river
there are no words nor mouth there are no words
and you die to forget the sleepless earth

Cut tongue with the taste of salt you weep my love
a light flower of the desert you bow your weary head
and we digest the blood forgotten we digest the blood
because you abandoned me forgotten desert
once more in the mouth

Cut tongue on the floor the twilight desert
the death that you watch is a sterile seed without you
I am nobody death after death we descend
and we descend without the memory there are no words
as there are no eyes they are pupils in the desert
you merely gaze absorbed the dilated shadows
of the blood curd

PECAT ORIGINAL

No tens voluntat i bandejat marxes
confós per l'expulsió, avergonyit
de ser tan feble, vas al teu pas bíblic.

N'esperaven massa de la primera
fornada. Ella carrega amb el mort
per fer-t'ho més fàcil. No hi pensis més,

has deixat de participar i ets lliure
de patir dels ronyons i guardar rocs
a la faixa per si de cas rapinyen.

Res no esperis de la providència,
per algun altre motiu que no t'expliquen
han resolt que t'espavilis, i trontolles

d'un lloc a un altre, perdut amb l'estirp
arreplegada al teu voltant. T'atures.

Ens ho deus, és el mínim. Truca a la porta.

ORIGINAL SIN

You don't have the will and exiled, you go
confused by the expulsion, ashamed
of being so weak, you take the bible path.

We hoped for too much of the first
lot. She carried death with her
to make it much easier. Don't dwell on it,

you have stopped engaging and are free
of the spine's pain and keep stones
in your pockets should violence come.

Expect nothing of providence,
for some motive you were not told
they decided you try harder, so you stagger

from one side to another, lost with the bloodline
gathered around you. You stop yourself

It's the least you owe them. Knock the door.

DIANA

Aquesta ha de ser la teva. No pot tan lluny
vibrar-ne cap altra. Tensa la corda i flexible
l'arquer atura l'esguard, quan potser, la memòria
de cada instant t'amaga perspectiva. Salten
les pors en mil pètals. No ets el covard que tem
les conseqüències i tibes encara més.
Hauràs d'anar al lloc comú on rígid tremoles
i no al sac dels que exhalen abans del dany. Fletxa
que just ara et parteix l'ombra per la meitat.

DIANA

It has to be yours. No other so far off could
flicker like that. He tautens the cord and supple
the archer holds the gaze, when, maybe, the memory
of each moment conceals perspective. It starts
fear in a thousand petals. You are not the coward who dreads
the consequences so you strain a little more. You must
seek the common ground where the rigid tremble,
not the sack with those who flinch before the blow.
Then an arrow cleaves your shadow in two.

CAMARADA NIN *Maig de 1937*

Proclamen el bell i pur estoïcisme a l'arbre
florit que incita al gaudi harmoniós i lent;
l'estat qualitatiu de la noblesa humana.

Com monstres que em voldrien buidar els ulls, tornen
nombrosos els cants a la branca més florida.

Me'ls miro escèptic i, caut, n'escolto el ressò:
la ingènua flor que espicassen a l'arbre mut.

COMRADE NIN *May of 1937*

Proclaim beauty and the pure stoic in the tree
flowering, that invites a slow harmonious bliss;
the qualitative state of noble humankind.

Like monsters who want to gouge out eyes, resurge
profusely in song to the most florid branch.

I study them sceptical, and cautiously, note their echo:
the naive flower they peck in the mute tree.

ALERTA

Renunciar perquè Déu ens arreplegui
no és mala idea.
                    Escriu Stevens:
"Tots els homes són assassins". Res
no modifica l'obra i vas tort
pensant que per no arribar ja caus.
Calen moltes vides per resoldre
els enunciats, i aquesta remor
de perill ve del dia d'abans
de néixer. La perceps entre els marges,
intranquil de no entendre la ruta.
Que bruts van els monstres, no descansen.

ALERT

To surrender so God can gather us up
is not a bad idea.
                    Stevens writes:
"All men are murderers". Nothing
modifies his work and you go askew
thinking that for not reaching you fall.
Many lives are required to settle
the statement, and this rumour
of danger comes the day before
birth. You perceive it between the margins
uneasy, not knowing the route.
The monsters are so grimy and can't rest.

FERIDA OBERTA

Ferida oberta, amb la sang rajada
et drenares en mi
cap a nosaltres.

Per un instant,
vàrem ser el mateix arbre;
dues boques superposades,
sense cap arrel.

Mal
encara
en el crit.

OPEN WOUND

Open wound, with the blood seeping
you drained me of
and to each.

For a single moment,
We went to the same tree;
two mouths one on the other
without any root.

evil
residual
in the scream

INVOLUCIÓ

Mal que obri l'aigua
i dipositi els ous d'amfibi
sota els còdols.

Mal que sota el marbre es congelin els ous
i llisqui per l'ombra
del meu fill.

Que l'arbre, del teu estrat
s'obri de fulles.
Silenci, a l'arrel de l'aigua.

Silenci, que es trenca la closca
i neixen contra l'arrel,
d'un estrat a l'altre.

INVOLUTION

Evil that parts the water
and deposits the frog spawn
beneath the gravel.

Evil that freezes the eggs beneath the marble
and slips by the shadow
of my son.

That the tree, of your layer
opens in leaf.
Silence, in the roots of the water.

Silence, that breaks the husk
and growing pushes out the root,
layer by layer.

LES ÀNIMES

N' hi ha que són brusques, o bé poc delicades,
en la pell llustrosa s'ufana el pur reflex
del llamp que sembla un calfred.

                                       D'altres més serenes
són marbre blanc plenes de vetes bondadoses,
raspen les mans fins ferir-les de buit.
Com viure
lluny de tocar-les?

                           Existeixen les tangibles
entre l'objecte i l'ombra, sempre a la mateixa
distància d' un cos extrem.

                                 No els cal res més,
quan és del tacte que davalla un final propi.

Hi ha alguna cosa més, diuen, però ja no hi són.

THE SOULS

The only ones are brusque, or better lacking tact
on glistening skin that boasts a pure reflection
of rays identical to a cold sweat.

                                    Others more serene
are white marble riven with a kind streak,
scratching their hands until it comes up vacuum.

                            How do we live
so far from their touch?

                            The tangibles exist
between the object and the shadow, always the same
distance from an external body.

                                They don't require any more
when they descend to a happy ending, touch.

There are more things, they say, but now they are gone.

GUEPARD

De l'organça espolinada al tafetà de seda
fa lluir la blonda ingràvida per les randes
de flocs daurats.
              Les models remuguen a la cua
de la bellesa. La lleugeresa dels vestits es mouen
al ritme lent d'un ball de passarel·la de moda,
marquen la tendència pels qui, fora del somni,
van evocant l'erotisme del maniquí virolat
i sospesen la cadència gràcil de cada passa:
del taló alt a la mida del cos perfecte. Així
el guepard indolent, que desafia les càmeres de fotos
detallistes que el van apuntant, quan l'esplendor
de l'automat somriu, i ella s'afirma. Llavors
preparats per capturar-la,
                            molt quiets.

CHEETAH

From organza woven into taffeta of silk
glistens the doily weightless for the lace
of golden flakes.
              The models murmur in the queue
of beauty. The levity of the dresses is stirred
by the slow rhythm of the dance of the catwalk,
a marked propensity which, for those outside the dream,
evokes the eroticism of the strident mannequin
and balances the graceful cadence of each step:
from high heel to the measure of the perfect body. So
the nonchalant cheetah defies the cameras
of the detail they are aiming for, when the splendor
of the automaton smiles, and she reaffirms. Then
we prepare to capture her,
                            almost stock-still.

OTTO DIX

Dels soldats mutilats que venen mistos
en un carrer fantasmal on les putes
riuen com bruixes i ensenyen deformades
les mamelles enormes de la pàtria.

A les esgarrinxades dels filferrats,
l'incendi de la mitja cara grisa
que enfosqueix l'altra en doble humiliació
pel paisatge erosionat: el buit jove.

Quanta indiferència crema en el vell
que amaga la calba per concentrar-se,
impotent en cavalcar un futur
que no li correspon. El coit fa mal.

OTTO DIX

From soldier amputees out hawking matches
in a phantom street where whores
snigger like witches and bare deformities,
the bloated tits of the fatherland.

To the gouges of the barbed wire fence
the fire of the half-seen ashen face
that hides a double shame
of eroded landscape: the vacant youth.

How much indifference burns in the patriarch
who holds his bald head down to get it up,
too feeble to mount a future
not his own. Sex hurts.

CINQUANTA

No és per tremolar, però aquí fa fred
i se't fica als ossos. El cor batega?

Difícil recordar-se'n, carregues
amb els anys definit al dibuix
del gargot que vas omplir de ratlles.

Ara l'infant, -el jutge cruel
que va preferir del joc les regles
inventades- ha marxat per sempre.

El paper groguenc és la distància
i el llapis buit de mina, el frec.
Orfe ho subrratlles, i t'esgarrifes.

FIFTY

It doesn't warrant tremors, but here it freezes
and gets into the bones. Does your heart skip?

Difficult to remember, burdened
with the years defined in the picture
of the doodle you filled up with lines

Now the boy - cruel judge
who once preferred the game to the rules
invented - has gone forever

The yellowing paper is the distance
and a pencil without lead, the smudge.
Orphaned, you underline it, and you shiver.

FIGURACIONS

Des de sempre que ho has volgut clar.
L'horitzó que degotes a la resina
s'estampa al paper en colors vius i brolla
de l'excepció. Veus de prop les flors policromes
que amb fel de bou i olis has fet escampar.
Vigila, no s'agrumollin els relleus
perceptibles. Llima'ls, tot just s'asequin.
La proporció no ha de semblar-te forçada.
Res no trobaràs més clar. L'instint busca
satisfer-se en els detalls: la embriaguesa.

GO FIGURE

You have clearly wanted this since forever.
The horizon that drips into the resin,
ground into the paper in bright colours breaks
bar none. Close up, you see the polychrome flowers
of ox bile and oils you are compelled to spread.
Be sure stark splodges don't clutter
the relief. Sand them down when dry.
The proportion doesn't seem to have been forced.
Nothing is more clear. Instinct seeks
satisfaction in detail which intoxicates.

EUFEMISME

Vinc de l'altra banda i sempre trigo.
I corro, i de lluny, transporto els vestigis
de l'antiga promesa.
         No tornessis
amb les mans buides, que càndid rebries
de valent.
         Aquesta és terra d'arreu,
on cada ombra viatja la distància
del vent que l'ha conreat. La dispersió
que també suma. Tossut l'arrossego
corrent amunt, mentre esquivo les soques
de l'albereda talada, i no bado,
que cauria l'enyor de tots. Venim.

EUPHEMISM

I come from elsewhere, and am always late
and race, and from afar, I bring the traces
of an ancient promise.
         Don't you return
empty-handed, or else you'll get one hell
of a beating.
         This is the earth be it from near or far
where every shadow travels in the distance
of the wind which ploughs it. A dispersion
that also adds up. Stubbornly, I haul it
upstream, while I avoid the vines
of the wooded grove, and I do not get distracted
but succomb to yearning like the others . We come.

A

Han encès la foscor. No ens hi veiem.
Als ulls, només pugen els tons grisencs:
gris plata, gris asfalt, gris hipopòtam.
Indigna el greuge, la manca d'hipnosi,
la droga de la interpretació bífida
que perfora el clapoteig permanent
dels ànecs. Així, quan calles tot calla,
el bec i l'aigua ensordits, encerclats
per anells que les plomes expandeixen,
un silenci pentinat ens va omplint
de volums que imagino poc estables.
Topem incòmodes, no pot ser lluny,
si apaguem la foscor la podrem veure.

A

They have lit the darkness. We don't watch.
To their eyes rise only shades of grey
grey plate, grey asphalt, grey hippo.
Indignant at the hurt, the lack of hypnosis,
the drug of the interpretation bifida
that perforates the permanent bubbling
of the ducks. So when you shut up, everyone shuts
their mouth and the deafening water, enclosed
by rings that the feathers expand,
a combed silence that fills us up
with volumes we imagine are unstable.
We find ourselves uncomfortable, we can't walk far
If we turn off the darkness, we will see it.

GUILLEM TELL/WILLIAM TELL

NÓOS

Els tenistes han vingut a maltractar les gallines i no els fa por la derrota que endevinen imminent. A cops de raqueta comproven que els ous no reboten i continuament cauen al terra del corral. Histriònics, no paren de riure, ampliant l'orgia malèfica que indueix el desordre a l'alteració del reglament. La responsabilitat del micròfon cavalca l'eco de la balena a les pastures de plàncton, però la fam no discrimina. Com grinyola el penell a la sala d'espera de l'inhòspit jutjat, segons bufa el vent els comdemna o els absol. Totes les gallines corren al voltant de la corona i la deixen perduda d'excrement i plomes.

NÓOS

The Tennis players have come to scare the hens, and it's not for fear of an imminent defeat. For a knockabout, they check the eggs don't bounce as they ceaselessly fall to the barnyard floor. Histrionics never cease to make them laugh and hearten the wicked orgy that induces disorder, alterations in the rules. The responsibility of the microphone rides the whale's echo to plankton pastures, but hunger does not discriminate. From the waiting room of the forbidding court, how the weather vane squeals; it condemns or absolves depending on the wind. All the hens run around the crown as it disappears under shit and feathers.

CANT DE DIONÍS

Amb el llevataps perfores la galàxia. Quan arribis a Epsilon Eridani recorda el nom de cada planeta. Cap suro és prou espès per desviar l'espiral de l'òrbita. Després del descens, l'elevació. El mussol amb les ales esteses que empeny avall, en un vol que busca el límit impossible, l'ebrietat.

DIONYSUS'S SONG

With a corkscrew, you can tap a galaxy. When you reach Epsilon Eridani, remember the name of each planet. No cork is dense enough to send the orbit off its spiral. After the descent, the ascension. The owl, its wings oustretched, pushes downwards, on its course for the impossible frontier: inebriation.

DRET A DECIDIR

Un home nu, amb els calçotets a la mà, salta penosament de la finestra. La inspiració és el salt que fa possible deixar-se la pell en la imatge furtiva de la carrera. Sospitós de trencar les normes, llença els calçotets als gossos que l'encalcen. En el fons, o ho intentes o te'n surts. Les condicions no es pacten i són les que et vas trobant a l'atzar. Aprens que la victòria esdevé la moral d'una èpica despullada. I corres decidit, veloç, sobre totes les derrotes.

RIGHT TO DECIDE

A naked man, with his underpants in his hand, struggles to leap from a window. Inspiration is the jump which lets him imprint his skin on the furtive image of the road. Suspected of breaking the norms, he kicks his underpants to the dogs giving him chase. Deep down, you try or you get lucky. The conditions are not right; you will find them at random. You learn that victory becomes the moral of a stark epic. And swift, steadfast, you run over all your defeats.

FMI

Les rates coneixen un dialecte de la nostra intimitat. No ho fan per altruisme, ni per convicció perversa. De fet saben que, com els cucs de terra, deixem tones ingents de matèria orgànica. No els importa que elaborem música, o refinades peces d'art, o commovedores evocacions nostàlgiques de gran bellesa elegíaca: les delicadeses no estimulen la fam dels rosegadors, no és la plusvàlua que de nosaltres esperen. Per elles, existim només per produir femta.

FMI

The rats know the idiom of our intimacy. Not out of altruism or a perverse conviction. In truth, they sense us by what we leave behind, like earthworms expelling organic matter. They don't care for the music we make, refined works of art, or moving evocations of a lost elegiac beauty. Delicacies do not sate the rodent desire. They do not esteem what we hold out for. To them, we exist just to shit.

MAIG 68

Les ungles pintades corren més que les mans a la illa de la revolució assistida. La clau anglesa cargola la boira: respirem malestar. Alguns escriuen llibres, d'altres es tiren pets. Glòria de la glòria, el son arreplega l'ara mateix i és millor que la invenció d'existir. Existir i observar la realitat, enorme, com s'estén al prat de búfals entre una polseguera indòmita. La lenta digestió que topa amb l'esterilitat del conjunt. Quants peus poden fer un camí? L'amor de debò és una desgràcia.

MAY' 68

Painted nails run faster than hands on the island of the bolstered revolution. Spanners screw the fog up tight; a malaise that we inhale. Some pen tracts, others pass gas. From glory to glory, sleep racks up the moment outshining the invention of existence. To exist and observe reality in its immensity extending out to the meadow of buffalo among an indomitable dust cloud. Slow digestion shadowing the whole's sterility. How many feet to forge a path? Love that must is a disgrace.

LLUISSOR

Observo el dibuix tècnic dels avions en un cel clar. Hi ha una teologia subratllada de cotó-fluix a la placenta de l'infinit. Com podem conservar les tangents? La geometria dels angles imaginaris acaba per diluir-se i penso en Alexandre reculant per la vall de l'Indo, insatisfet, derrotat pel seu propi exèrcit. Va entendre que el somni es desfaria entre els trenats de les Moires, car mai no veuria el seu rostre complet, pare d'ell mateix, en una matinada de mil sols que il·luminessin, com avui, el seient de passatgers del vol New York- Barcelona, cosint el paisatge facial amb la mà oberta, com una aranya que cobreix la finestra del món, i el fa, per un moment, reconeixible.

RADIANCE

Observe this technical drawing of planes in a clear sky. How can we preserve the tangents? The geometry of imaginary angles melts away. And I think of Alexander, retreating through the Indus valley, dissatisfied, defeated by his own army. He understood the dream would vanish between the weaving of the Fates, that he would never see his own face, he who fathered himself, on the morning of a thousand suns that illuminate like today, sat on a flight from Dehli to

New York, sewing the facial landscape with an open hand, like a spider that covers the window of the world, and doing so, leaves it recognizable, if only momentarily.

LLIÇÓ DE LINGÜÍSTICA

Mira fill, tots els verbs quan van junts avancen els esdeveniments imperceptibles, alguns s'amaguen als calaixos de la veritat –que és una forma de dir-. La convivència resta garantida pels majordoms del sentit comú. Sempre hi ha fronteres on vigilar els meteorits que travessen el cor de la nit, un espectacle digne de gegants, com una mena de fi del món sense importància. Però la sintaxi és el policia de la cara gravada per la llei, detalla les desviacions del sender als informes apocalíptics i confirma, així, l'aleació d'un nou metall en la descripció exhaustiva de la finestra. Commou sentir la veu de les virtuts amb els adjectius precisos, després del trànsit d'una realitat que mai no passarà de ser alguna cosa més que la certesa. Recorda això, fill, no deixis d'imaginar-t'ho.

LINGUISTIC LESSON

Look son, all the verbs when they come together advance imperceptible events; some squirrel away truth's chest of drawers - in a manner of speaking. Co-existence prevails, guaranteed by the butlers of common sense. There are always frontiers from which to watch the meteorites that cross the heart of the night like an end of the world without importance. But syntax polices the engraved face by law, detailing the deviations from the path to apocalyptic reports and, here, confirms the alloying of a new metal in the exhaustive description of the window. I swear to hear the voice of virtue with precise adjectives before a passing reality that will never be more than certain. Remember this, son, do not forget to imagine it.

IDENTITAT

No existim, Déu especula. I són ateus els qui neguen la imaginació, com són esclaus els creients que enceten obsessius el camí de l'ascesi. I si tots els camins fan marrada, que n'és de falsa la geometria del cor. L'ancià del gipó burell s'encarrega de donar la volta al rellotge d'arena, quan el grapat que resta de l'illeta s'escola coll avall a l'altre present, allà, on només existeixen els dos daus que reboten pels costats imprevisibles del món. De nosaltres, no en tenim ni puta idea.

IDENTITY

We do not exist, God speculates. And more that atheists are those who deny the imagination; believers, slaves whose very obsession sets them on the path of asceticism. And what if all the paths are detours, the geometry of colour a sham? The old man with the greying doublet is in charge of the hourglass's turning when what remains of the isle is scattered to another present there where nothing exists but two dice rebounding off the sides of an unknowable planet. Of ourselves, we don't have a fucking clue.

L'ULL QUE NOMÉS MIRA

L'ull que només mira la duresa de les formes i en tancar-se troba el dolor del vidre clavant-se en un milió de microagulles esmolades. Oh somni! Enfilall de sons encadenats, encavalcats en sèries infinites, que evoquen alternatives insòlites, la clau del desconcert en la freqüència de l'espasme, el parpelleig instaurat en l'esfondrament del llautó.

THE EYE THAT ONLY LOOKS UPON

The eye that only looks upon the hardness of the form upon closing only knows the pain like a million micro glass shards hammered in. Oh, What a dream! A wisp of intermingled sleep, looping infinitely, evoking far-flung answers, a key to bewilderment in the spasm's frequency, the restorative flicker of brass buckling under.

ARIZONA

Com un tornavís elèctric en lliscar per la superfície del formigó impenetrable, el tornado empeny el paisatge en enroscar-se. A l'horitzó treballen el transplantament de somriure, així resta segellada la fusió de dues oracions: una, enfurida, que puja i baixa per l'esòfag tubular de l'escala de Jacob, l'altra, que roman a la cicatriu del circuit. El somriure de l'agraïment calma la set de la gràcia eterna.

ARIZONA

Like an electric screwdriver slip-sliding off the concrete top, the tornado nudges the landscape as its tightens. On the horizon, it transplants smiles, there where the merging of two phrases fuse: one, in a fury, up and down the oesophagus of Jacob's ladder; the other that dwells in the scar's circuit. It's a smile of gratitude that calms the craving for eternal grace.

CAN RUTI

Viure a l'hospital de les patates fregides, invertebrat per politraumatismes irreversibles, i observar el tramat de les teranyines al vidre de la finestra. Sentir l'interval dels cops repetits. La sang dels bitxacs esclafats a la paret externa de l'hospital imprimeix d'expressionisme abstracte el paisatge. Arriba, però, el moment que entra l'aire invasiu, i el cruixent de les ones insinuades s'esbocina en engrunes i àtoms a la masticació de la memòria: el motiu és tenir plegats un bosc per recordar.

CAN RUTI

Go live in the hospital of potato crisps, those invertebrates with irreversible injuries. Observe the plaster of spider webbing on the window pane. Feel the interval of repeated blows. The blood of the goshawks crushed against the outer wall of the hospital leaves an imprint of a lanscape, abstract, expressionist. Above, however, once the invasive air enters; the crunch of insinuated waves break away into crumbs; and atoms into the chewing gum of memory, the motive is to have a forest to remember together.

Maurice Scully was born in Dublin in 1952 and spent his childhood between Clare, the Ring Gaeltacht, and Dublin. He was educated at Trinity College Dublin. He has been editor of a number of influential magazines (Icarus, The Beau), and through the 1970s and 1980s organised important readings and literary events.

In a writing career that began in the early 1970s he has published over a dozen volumes of poetry and taken part in conferences and festivals in Ireland, the UK, and the US, where his readings are prized as key interpretations of his complex, engaging work.

For 25 years Scully's work was devoted to a single vast project under the overall title of Things That Happen which consists of 5 Freedoms of Movement, Livelihood, Sonata, and Tig, the coda to the whole work. See his publications here.

After many years living in Italy, Africa and the west of Ireland, he settled with his wife and four children in Dublin, where he taught for a time at Dublin City University. He is a member of Aosdána.

Jordi Valls Pozo is a Catalan poet who has lived in Santa Coloma de Gramenet, a city that strongly influenced his poetic trajectory for the majority of his life. He was president of the Associació de Joves Escriptors en Llengua Catalana (Association of Young Catalan Language Writers) from 1994 to 1996 and is a member of The Associació d'Escriptors en Llengua Catalana (AELC) and The PEN Club Català (Catalan PEN Club).

Having won The Jocs Florals de la Llengua Catalana in 2006, he was the first author to hold the office of City Poet. Ernest Farrés, editor of the anthology *21 poetes del XXI* (2001), states that "In the hands of Jordi Valls poetry is not only subversion but it is most of all the essence of the literary fact".

He has read at: Days of poetry and wine, Medana, Slovenia 2008, Encuentro Internacional de Poesía Ciudad de México 2015, Festival International Poetry Bucharest 2017, Festival de Poesía "Luna de Locos" Pereira, Colombia, 2017.

Raoul Izzard is an English teacher who has settled in Barcelona with his wife, Susana, baby son, Pau, and dog, June dog. He says that poetry is one of the best ways he has found to create. He loves to read it, write it, and hear it performed.

www.ingramcontent.com/pod-product-compliance
Lightning Source LLC
Chambersburg PA
CBHW031935080426
42734CB00007B/696